EVERYTHING ORIGAMI

ORIGAMI ANIMALS

Matthew Gardiner

WINDMILL
BOOKS

New York

Published in 2016 by **Windmill Books,**
an Imprint of Rosen Publishing
29 East 21st Street, New York, NY 10010

Editor: Katie Hewat
Graphic Designer: My Trinh Gardiner
Origami Artists: Darren Scott, Jonathan Baxter, Steven Casey

Cataloging-in-Publication Data
Gardiner, Matthew.
Origami animals / by Matthew Gardiner.
p. cm. — (Everything origami)
Includes index.
ISBN 978-1-4777-5623-2 (pbk.)
ISBN 978-1-4777-5622-5 (6 pack)
ISBN 978-1-4777-5546-4 (library binding)
1. Origami — Juvenile literature. 2. Animals in art — Juvenile literature. I. Title.
TT870.G373 2016
736'.982—d23

Manufactured in the United States of America
CPSIA Compliance Information: Batch # WS15WM: For Further Information contact Rosen Publishing, New York, New York at 1-800-237-9932

CONTENTS

Symbols

Lines

----·---·---·----	Mountain fold (crease forms a ridge)		– – – –	Valley fold (crease forms a trough)	
···············	X-ray or projection (can be hidden valley or mountain)		————	Crease	

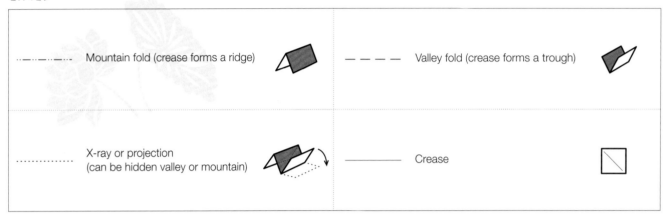

Arrows

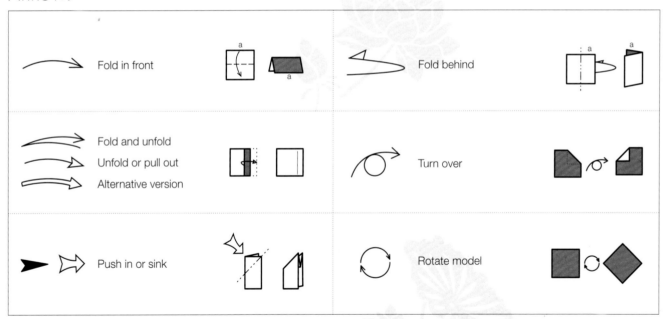

	Fold in front			Fold behind	
	Fold and unfold			Turn over	
	Unfold or pull out				
	Alternative version				
	Push in or sink			Rotate model	

Extras

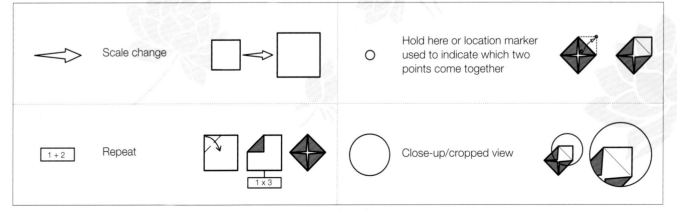

	Scale change		○	Hold here or location marker used to indicate which two points come together	
1 + 2	Repeat	1 x 3	○	Close-up/cropped view	

TYPES OF FOLDS

BOOK FOLD

Valley fold one edge to another, like closing a book.

CUPBOARD FOLD

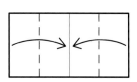

Fold both edges to the middle crease, like closing two cupboard doors.

BLINTZ

Fold all corners to the middle. This was named after a style of pastry called a blintz.

PLEAT

A mountain and valley fold combination.

BISECT –

DIVIDE A POINT IN TWO

Many folds use a corner and two edges to position the fold line. The most common is a bisection, or division of an angle in two.

Fold one edge to meet the other, making sure the crease goes through the corner.

INSIDE REVERSE FOLD

The spine of the existing fold is reversed and pushed inside.

OUTSIDE REVERSE FOLD

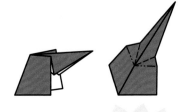

The spine of the existing fold is reversed and wrapped outside.

DOUBLE REVERSE

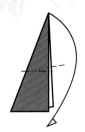

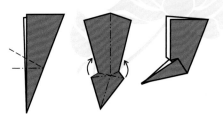

A double reverse fold is two reverse folds made in sequence on the same point.

The last diagram shows the paper slightly unfolded, to illustrate the folds that are made.

INSIDE CRIMP   OUTSIDE CRIMP

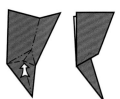

Crimps are often used for making feet or shaping legs. They can be thought of as a pleat mirrored on both sides of the point.

An inside crimp tucks the pleat on the inside of the point.

An outside crimp wraps the pleat over the outside of the point.

PETAL FOLD   The petal fold is found in the bird and lily base.

1   2   3   4   5

Fold top layer to the center crease.

Fold and unfold the top triangle down. Unfold flaps.

Lift the top layer upwards.

Step 3 in progress, the model is 3D. Fold the top layer inwards on existing creases.

Completed petal fold.

SQUASH   A squash fold is the symmetrical flattening of a point. The flattening movement is known as squashing the point.

1   2   3   4

Pre-crease on the line for the squash fold.

Open up the paper by inserting your finger. Fold the paper across.

As you put the paper in place, gently squash the point into a symmetrical shape.

Completed squash fold.

OPEN SINK

1

Pre-crease through all layers along the sink line. It's best to make a mountain and a valley fold on this line.

2

Open out the point, and push the point into the paper. Take care to reverse folds as shown. The sink should squash flat.

3

Completed sink.

RABBIT EAR   The rabbit ear fold is named after a most useful shape – that of a rabbit ear. It is used to make a new point.

1

2

3

1- 3. Divide each corner of the triangle with valley folds.

4

Fold top edges to the bottom, the middle crease will form a point.

5

Fold the point to one side.

6

Completed rabbit ear.

DOUBLE RABBIT EAR   The double rabbit ear is a rabbit ear fold that is mirrored on both sides of the point.

1

Make a rabbit ear fold on the point.

2

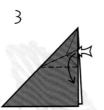

Unfold the rabbit ear.

3

Squash fold the point.

4

Inside reverse fold the two points.

5

Valley fold point upwards.

6

Completed double rabbit ear.

SWIVEL FOLD

A swivel fold is often made on a pleat. It narrows its two points, and the excess paper swivels under one of the points.

MANDARIN DUCK

The Mandarin duck is inspired by a traditional model. The Mandarin duck is a migratory bird, and flies to southern China and Japan during the winter months. The male Mandarin duck has very distinctive patterning on its head, so use a decorative sheet of paper.

A Chinese proverb relates loving couples to "two Mandarin ducks playing in water."

1

Start with white side up. Fold and unfold diagonal.

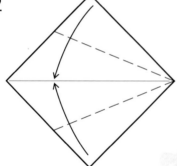

2

Fold both sides to the middle.

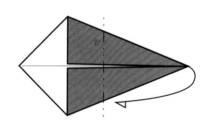

3

Mountain fold in half behind.

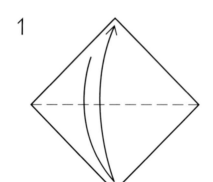

4

Squash fold both sides.

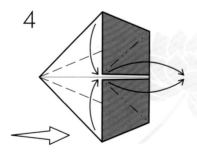

5

Mountain fold the back layer behind.

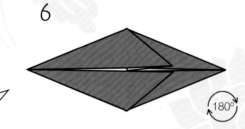

6

This is known as the fish base. Rotate 180°.

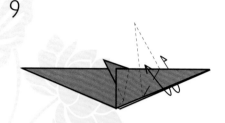

7

Fold top half behind.

8

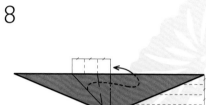

Double reverse fold small flaps.
Repeat behind.

9

Outside reverse right point.

10

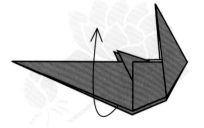

Lift layer upward.

11

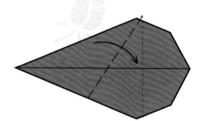

Fold top edge in line with dotted
vertical line.

12

Unfold.

13

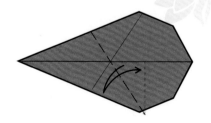

Repeat in other direction.

14

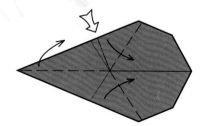

Rabbit ear on existing creases.

15

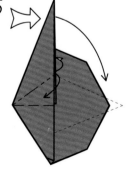

Lift the point upwards and squash fold.

16

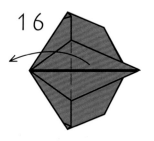

Valley fold the top point to the left.

17

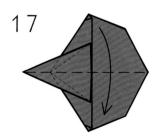

Fold top half down in front.

18

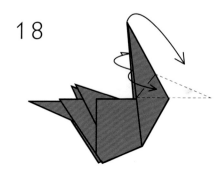

Outside reverse.

19

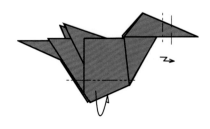

Fold bottom edge under and into body.
Double reverse point to form bill.

20

Completed Mandarin duck.

LABRADOR

The Labrador is a smart dog: obedient, energetic, affectionate, and faithful. Use a large sheet 12 inches (30 cm) or larger of black, brown or golden paper to make your favorite colored Labrador.

The Labrador breed is so intelligent and reliable that they make up about 60% of all guide dogs.

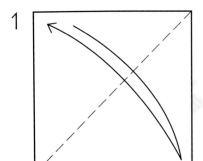

1

Begin white side up.
Fold and unfold diagonal.

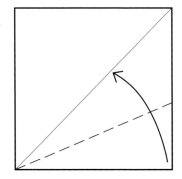

2

Fold bottom edge to diagonal crease.

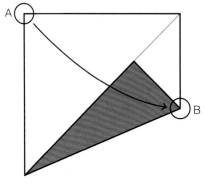

3

Fold point A to point B, make a small crease at top.

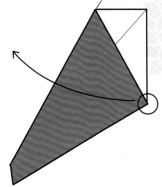

4

The top left corner marks one third.

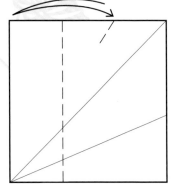

5

Fold the edge to meet the third.

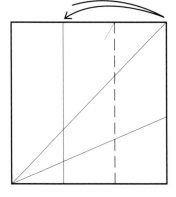

6

Fold the other edge to meet fold from step 5.

7

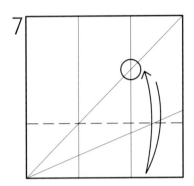

Fold the bottom edge to meet the marked intersection, then unfold.

8

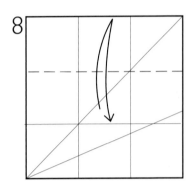

Fold top edge to meet fold from step 7.

9

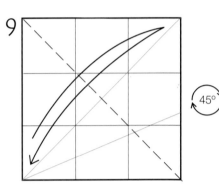

Fold and unfold diagonal. Rotate 45°.

10

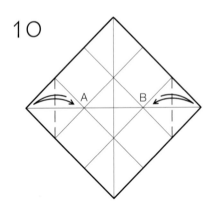

Fold side corners to points A and B then unfold.

11

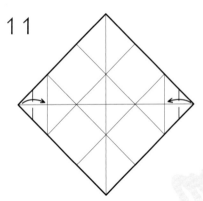

Fold side corners to crease made in step 10.

12

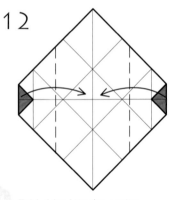

Fold sides into the center.

13

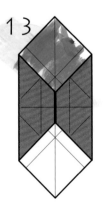

Rotate model 90°.

14

Mountain fold top half behind.

15

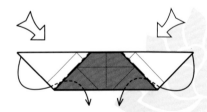

Reverse fold side flaps. Next step changes scale.

16

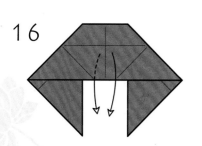

Fold single flaps down in front and behind.

17

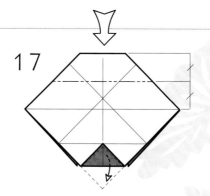

Sink top section. Unfold the corner from behind.

18

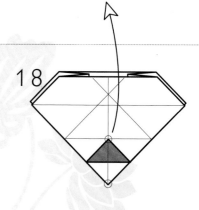

Hold lower corner and pull upper corner to open out model completely. Scale is reduced next step.

19

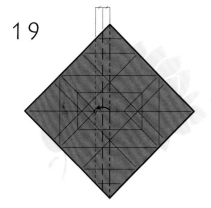

Add a diagonal pleat.

20

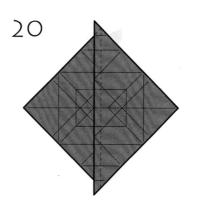

Turn over top to bottom.

21

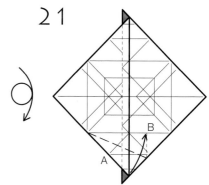

Fold edge A to crease B.

22

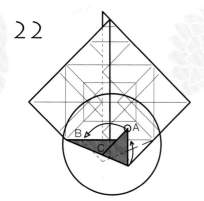

Grab point A and rotate until it touches raw edge B. Corner C drops down.

23

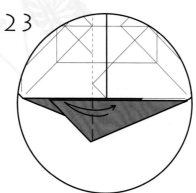

Pre-crease.

24

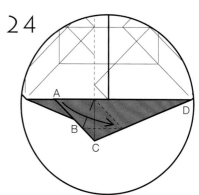

Fold point A to touch the diagonal line C-D. The line A-B should be horizontal.

25
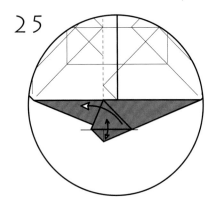
Pre-crease lower edge. Unfold the upper flap.

26
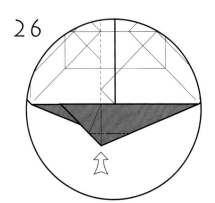
Sink lower edge.

27
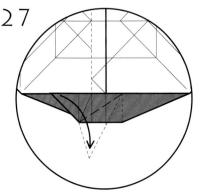
Fold flap down. The layers behind separate and flatten.

28
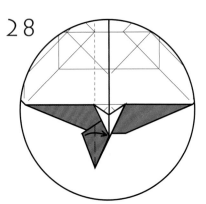
Valley fold to narrow flap. Next step shows full view.

29
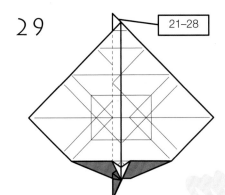
21–28

Repeat steps 21–28 on the top half of the model.

30
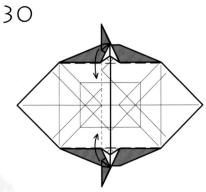
Valley fold top and bottom sections inward.

31
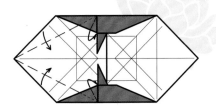
Swivel fold.

32
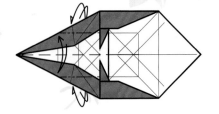
Add some additional creases.

33
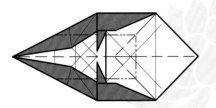
Collapse using existing creases.

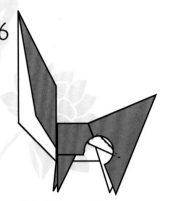

34

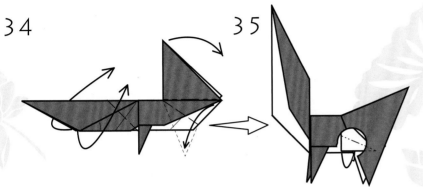

Outside reverse fold. Crimp right flaps down.

35

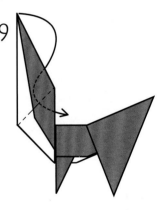

Cutaway view: Bisect inside triangle and then reverse fold.

36

This is the result.

37

Cutaway view: Reverse fold inside corner. Repeat on other side.

38

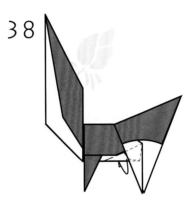

Fold lower flap up into the body. Repeat on other side.

39

Reverse fold head section.

40

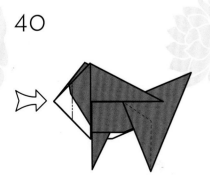

Open sink.

41

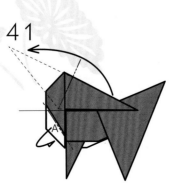

Reverse fold head point. Tuck flap A into body. Repeat on other side.

42

Tuck flap up into body. Outside reverse fold head.

43

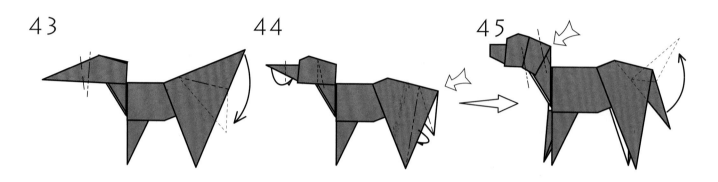

Double reverse fold to form muzzle.
Reverse fold tail.

44

Add crimp to form ears. Narrow tail and
legs with a swivel fold. Inside reverse
fold to shorten the nose.

45

Reverse fold tail, and use inside reverse
folds to shape ears.

46

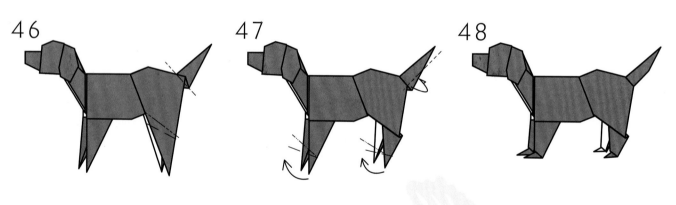

Tuck in flap at base of tail.
Crimp hind legs.

47

Crimp all feet. Narrow tail.

48

Completed Labrador.

MOUSE

The mouse is a member of the rodent family. This mouse resembles the well-known common house mouse, with alert ears and a long tail. Attempt this model first with a 12-inch (30 cm) sheet before progressing onto a smaller sheet size for a life-size mouse.

The mouse is regarded as the third most successful mammal on the planet, due to its ability to adapt to almost any environment.

1

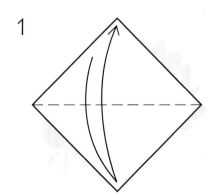

Begin white side up.
Fold and unfold diagonal.

2

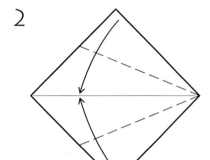

Fold both sides to the middle.

3

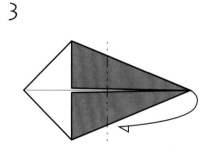

This is known as the kite base.
Mountain fold in half.

4

Squash fold both sides.

5

Mountain fold the point behind.

6

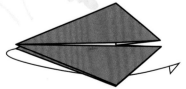

This is known as the fish base.
Rotate 90°.

7

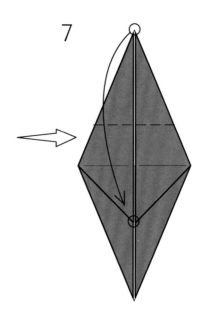

Fold the top down to the tip of the small triangles.

8

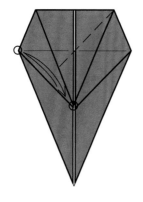

Bring the middle point to the outside corner then unfold.

9

Repeat step 8 in the other direction.

10

Unfold point to original position.

11

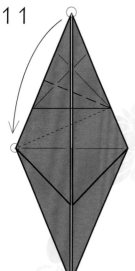

Fold tip down to corner.

12

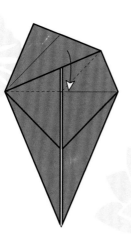

Ease out extra paper.

13

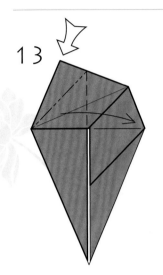

Fold the top layer across, to make a squash fold on the top point.

14

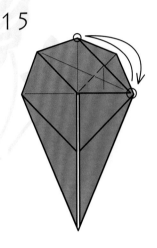

Pull out extra paper.

15

Pre-crease.

16

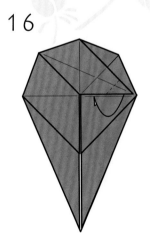

Inside reverse.

17

Do another inside reverse fold.

18

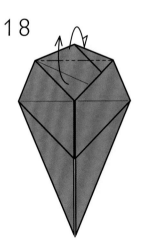

Flip back.

19

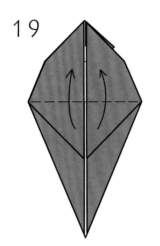

Valley fold small flaps up.

20

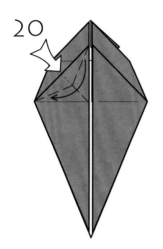

Rabbit ear the top layer.

21

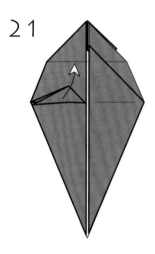

Unfold the rabbit ear.

22

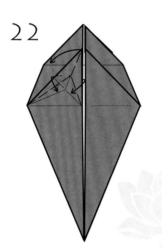

Add a new rabbit ear around the creases of the original. Place the tip near the side corner.

23

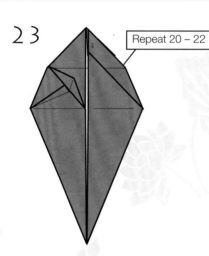

Repeat 20 – 22

Repeat the folds on the right-hand flap.

24

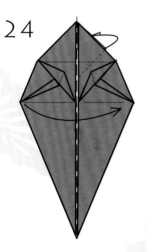

Fold in half. Allow hidden flap on the right to flip behind to the left.

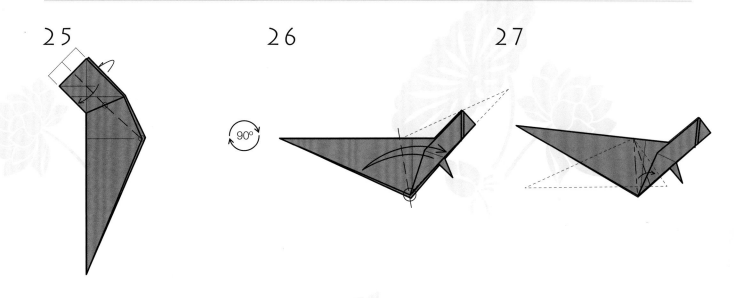

25

Valley fold in front, mountain fold behind. Rotate to position in next step.

26

90°

Fold the lower left edge in line with the right. The crease runs through the lower corner.

27

Crimp back legs and tail section.

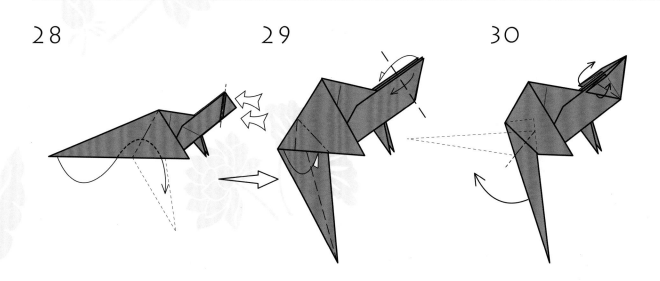

28

Reverse fold tail. Push in two corners.

29

Swivel fold tail on both sides. Fold ears back.

30

Reverse fold tail. Fold ear flaps forward.

31

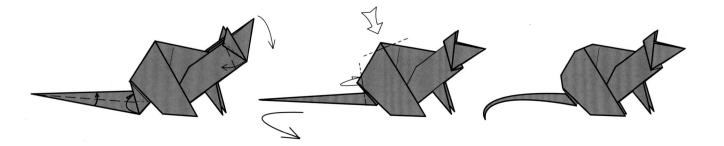

Crimp head down. Swivel fold tail.
Repeat behind.

32

Tuck the back points into the body and
close sink the top point. Curl the tail.

33

Completed mouse.

RABBIT

The rabbit is a small mammal found in many parts of the world. Rabbits have long ears which they use to listen for predators. This rabbit by Steven Casey has all four legs, a white tail and long ears. It is best folded from a 12-inch (30 cm) sheet or larger, as there are many detailed folds. Use a sheet with the same color on both sides to get a completely single-colored model.

The rabbit is a quick runner, and an even quicker breeder. Baby rabbits take only a month to gestate. A single rabbit can give birth to a normal size litter of seven babies about five times per year.

1

Begin white side up.
Fold and unfold diagonals. Turn over.

2

Book fold and unfold.

3

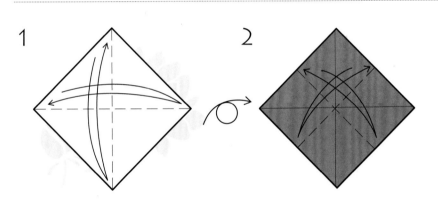

Bring three corners down to meet bottom corner. Start with corners 1 and 2 together followed by corner 3.

4

Rotate 180° so the open points are at the top. Fold single layer down then unfold.

5

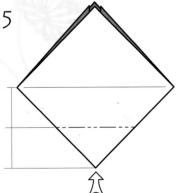

Pre-crease, then sink the bottom tip.

6

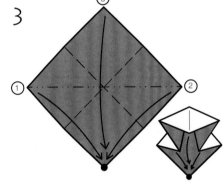

Valley fold upper layer and spread squash fold hidden corners.

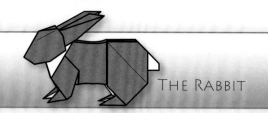
7

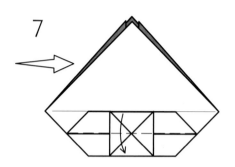

Fold upper layer down.

8

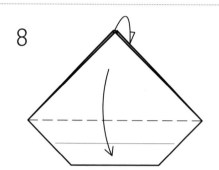

Fold single flap down in front and behind.

9

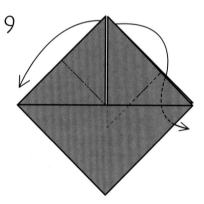

Reverse fold both points as shown.

10

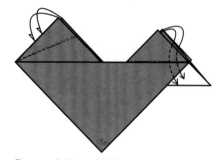

Reverse fold two left flaps
and two right flaps.

11

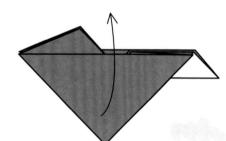

Fold single layer up.

12

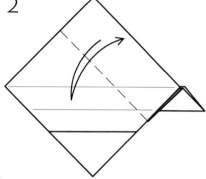

Pre-crease.

13

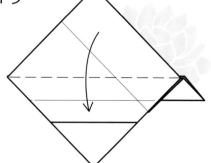

Valley fold top point down.

14

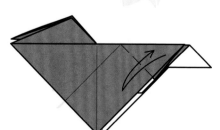

Fold triangle flap down, then unfold.

15

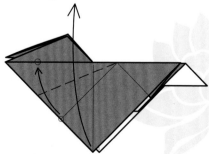

Bring points together with a valley fold.
The layer will become 3D.

16

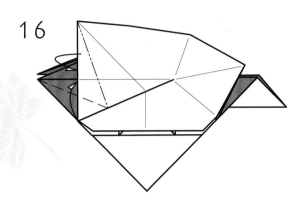

Swivel fold.

17

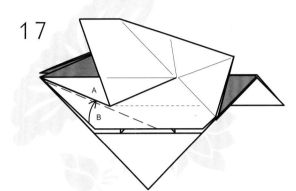

Tuck B under A.

18

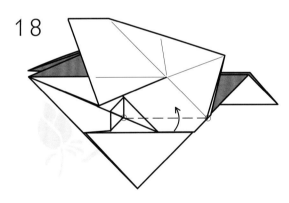

Valley fold edge inwards.

19

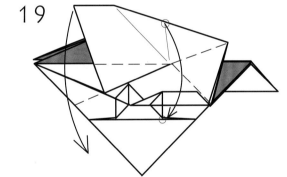

Bring the top flap down. Align the circled points.
At this stage the flap will not lie flat.

20

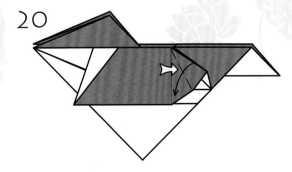

Push in where shown and fold the edge down
to meet the crease.

21

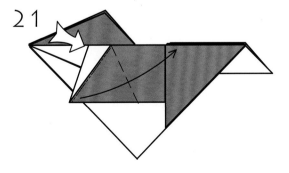

Squash fold.

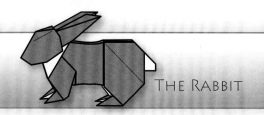
22

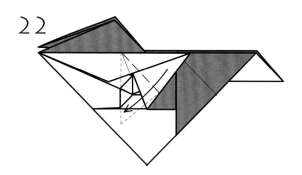

Fold flap down.

23

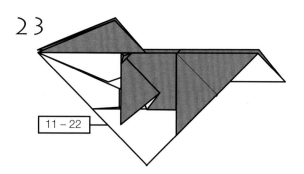

11 – 22

Repeat steps 11–22 behind.

24

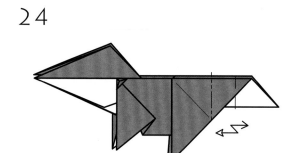

Pleat tail section then unfold.

25

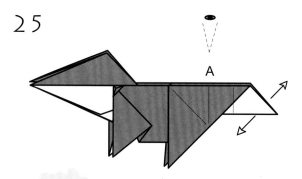

A

Open out tail section.

26

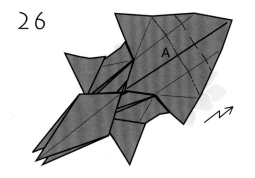

A

View from arrow A. Pleat tail section.

27

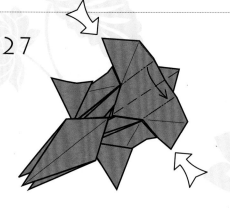

Push sides together.

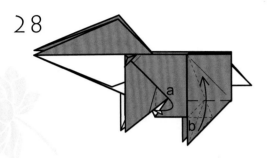

28

Push in corner A and lift flap B, squashing layers underneath.

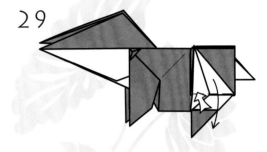

29

Fold upper flap back down.

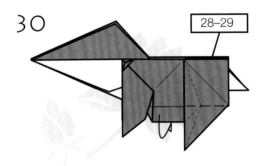

30

28–29

Repeat steps 28–29 behind. Fold flap under in line with inner edge. Repeat behind.

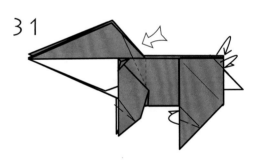

31

Sink the back of the head. Crimp front and back feet, and tuck in corners near tail.

32

Valley fold ear flaps. Shorten the tail with a reverse fold.

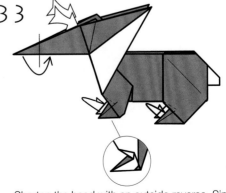

33

Shorten the head with an outside reverse. Sink the inner corners between the ears. Narrow the feet. Note the swivel that forms underneath.

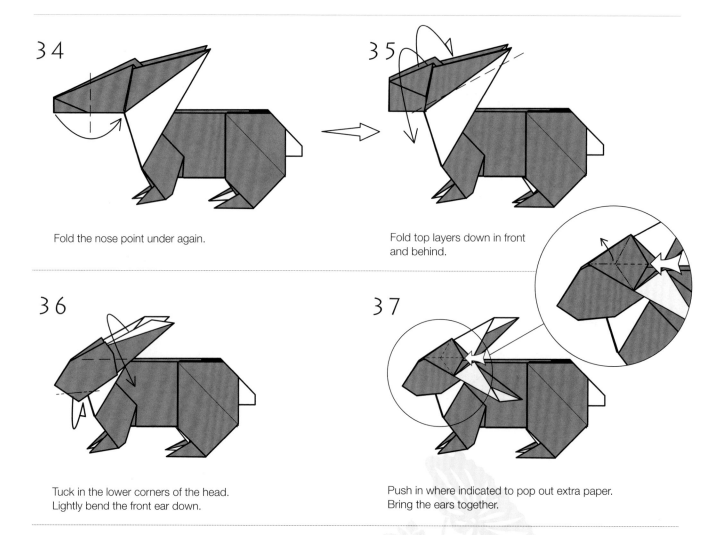

34

Fold the nose point under again.

35

Fold top layers down in front and behind.

36

Tuck in the lower corners of the head. Lightly bend the front ear down.

37

Push in where indicated to pop out extra paper. Bring the ears together.

38

Tuck the lower edges of the ears inside, repeat behind. Shape the body by pressing along the top and underside of the rabbit.

39

Completed rabbit.

TURTLE

The turtle is a member of the reptile family. Its bony shell gives it shelter from predators, and its webbed feet allow it to swim quickly in water, but still walk on land for nesting. Use a 12-inch (30 cm) or larger sheet for this model, as there are a few layers in the head and tail, and the details require more paper.

The turtle cannot breathe in water, but it can hold its breath for a long time.

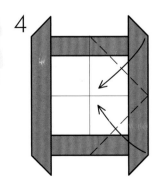

1

Begin white side up.
Book fold and unfold.

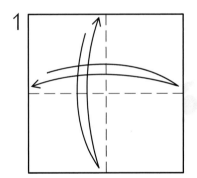

2

Fold each edge into the center then unfold.

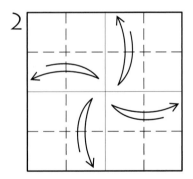

3

Fold edges in, and rabbit ear corners.

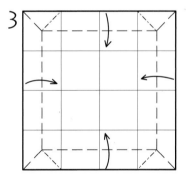

4

Fold right corners into center.

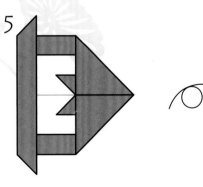

5

Completed step 4. Turn over.

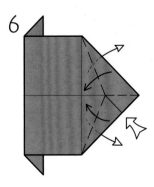

6

Rabbit ear on right side. Allow layers from behind to flip out.

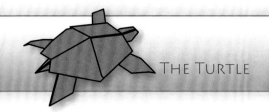

7

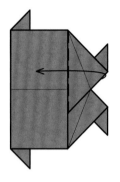

Fold single flap over to the left.

8

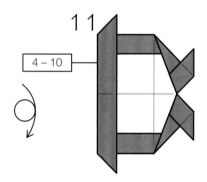

Fold small flap upwards.

9

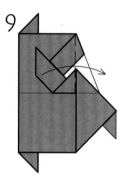

Fold flap over to the right.

10

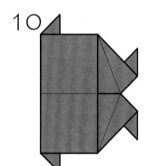

Turn over top to bottom.

11

4 – 10

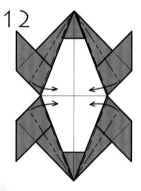

Repeat steps 4–10 on the left half of the model.

12

Crimp all four flaps.

13

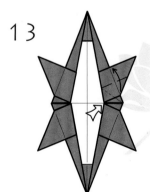

Squash fold.

14

13   13

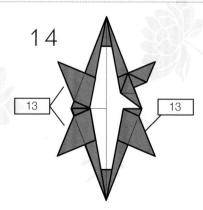

Repeat step 13 on remaining flaps.

15

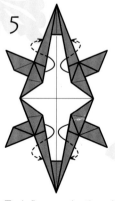

Tuck flaps under the white layer. The top flaps go between the small hidden flap and the white layer.

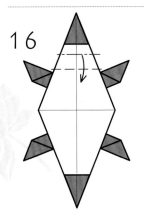

16

Pleat top point.

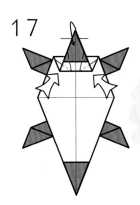

17

Squash fold corners. Valley fold the top
point down.

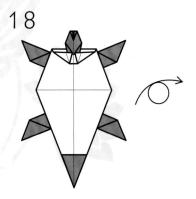

18

Turn over.

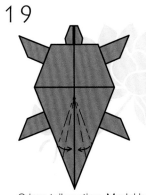

19

Crimp tail section. Model become 3D.

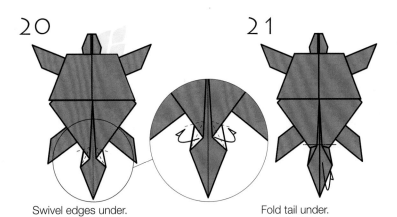

20

Swivel edges under.

21

Fold tail under.

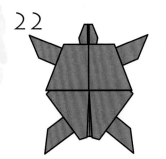

22

Completed step 21. Turn over.

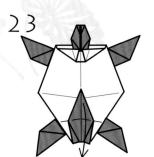

23

Valley fold tail. Turn over.

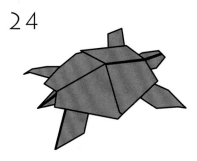

24

Completed turtle.

Glossary

AFFECTIONATE giving a feeling of love

GESTATE to carry unborn offspring internally during pregnancy

MAMMAL a warm-blooded animal that has a backbone and hair, breathes air, and feeds milk to its young

MIGRATORY moving to warmer or colder places for a season

OBEDIENT willing to obey

PREDATOR an animal that hunts other animals for food

RODENT a small, furry animal with large front teeth, such as a mouse or rat

WEBBED connected by skin

Index

For More Information

Palacios, Vicente. *Origami Animals*. Mineola, NY: Dover, 2012.

Woodroffe, David. *The Complete Book of Origami Animals*. London: Constable & Robinson, 2013.

For web resources related to the subject of this book, go to:
www.windmillbooks.com/weblinks and select this book's title.